The Peculiar Past in
ANCIENT ROME

by Charis Mather

BEARPORT
PUBLISHING

Minneapolis, Minnesota

Credits

All images are courtesy of Shutterstock.com, unless otherwise specified. With thanks to Getty Images, Thinkstock Photo, and iStockphoto.
Cover – VectorPlotnikoff, Macrovector, ProStockStudio, Mironov Konstantin. 4–5 – rararorro, Artem Avetisyan, Woeterman 94, CC BY-SA 3.0 <https://creativecommons.org/licenses/by-sa/3.0>, via Wikimedia Commons, NotionPic. 6–7 – Alfmaler, Planeta Vinilo, Kizel Cotiw-an, mm7, © José Luiz Bernardes Ribeiro, LynxVector, Victor Adam, Public domain, via Wikimedia Commons, Happy Job, HappyPictures. 8–9 – Gustav Wertheimer, Public domain, via Wikimedia Commons, National Printing & Engraving Company (U.S.); Kleine, George.; Cines (Firm)., Public domain, via Wikimedia Commons, ONYXprj, Jean Lombard (26 September 1854 – 17 July 1891), Public domain, via Wikimedia Commons, SofiaV, Darvi Odraid, Rvector. 10–11 – Clara Grosch, Public domain, via Wikimedia Commons, Henri De Montaut, Public domain, via Wikimedia Commons, PCH.Vector, Cesare Maccari, Public domain, via Wikimedia Commons, Vincenzo Camuccini, Public domain, via Wikimedia Commons, Drawlab19. 12–13 – meunierd, Vuk Kostic, Mariageorgieva0802, CC BY-SA 4.0 <https://creativecommons.org/licenses/by-sa/4.0>, via Wikimedia Commons, Rijksmuseum, CC0, via Wikimedia Commons, Bigmouse108, HappyPictures. 14–15 – Jean-Léon Gérôme, Public domain, via Wikimedia Commons, Nicolao Landucci, Public domain, via Wikimedia Commons, paul and paula, Mikko-Pekka Salo, Macrovector. 16–17 – Edwin Howland Blashfield, Public domain, via Wikimedia Commons, Look_Studio, Grimgram, Ulpiano Checa, Public domain, via Wikimedia Commons. 18–19 – Wellcome Images, CC BY 4.0 <https://creativecommons.org/licenses/by/4.0>, via Wikimedia Commons, 4zevar, Viktorija Reuta, Jean Lombard (26 September 1854 – 17 July 1891), Public domain, via Wikimedia Commons, By Lawrence Alma-Tadema - Superb magazine, The Désirs & Volupté exhibition at the Musée Jacquemart-André – direct link, Public Domain, https://commons. wikimedia.org/w/index.php?curid=755081, Guiin. 20–21 – Sabelskaya, Heracleitus, Public domain, via Wikimedia Commons, Sira Anamwong, Spreadthesign, exxxistence, svtdesign, Nezakat Kerimova 71, inspiring.team, Gustave Boulanger, Public domain, via Wikimedia Commons, Rvector, Artfury. 22–23 – Bernhard Keil, Public domain, via Wikimedia Commons, Incomible, Joseph-Noël Sylvestre, Public domain, via Wikimedia Commons. 24–25 – grmarc, Al-Tair, BlueRingMedia, Tomacco, Kastoluza, Roberto Bompiani, Public domain, via Wikimedia Commons, TyB, CC BY 2.0 <https://creativecommons.org/licenses/by/2.0>, via Wikimedia Commons, Nicolas Poussin, Public domain, via Wikimedia Commons, artbesouro, Net Vector. 26–27 – Carole Raddato from FRANKFURT, Germany, CC BY-SA 2.0 <https://creativecommons.org/ licenses/by-sa/2.0>, via Wikimedia Commons, AstralManSigmaDelta, fox_workshop, Macrovector, Elena Platova. 28–29 – Internet Archive Book Images, No restrictions, via Wikimedia Commons, ivector, Eduardo Ettore Forti, Public domain, via Wikimedia Commons, mentalmind. 30 – gashgeron.

Bearport Publishing Company Product Development Team
President: Jen Jenson; Director of Product Development: Spencer Brinker; Managing Editor: Allison Juda; Associate Editor: Naomi Reich; Associate Editor: Tiana Tran; Art Director: Colin O'Dea; Designer: Elena Klinkner; Designer: Kayla Eggert; Product Development Assistant: Owen Hamlin

Library of Congress Cataloging-in-Publication Data

Names: Mather, Charis, 1999- author.
Title: The peculiar past in ancient Rome / by Charis Mather.
Description: Minneapolis, Minnesota : Bearport Publishing, [2024] | Series: Strange history | Includes bibliographical references and index.
Identifiers: LCCN 2023044539 (print) | LCCN 2023044540 (ebook) | ISBN 9798889164807 (library binding) | ISBN 9798889164852 (paperback) | ISBN 9798889164890 (ebook)
Subjects: LCSH: Rome--Social life and customs--Anecdotes--Juvenile literature. | Rome--Biography--Anecdotes--Juvenile literature.
Classification: LCC DG78 .M3765 2024 (print) | LCC DG78 (ebook) | DDC 937--dc23/eng/20230922
LC record available at https://lccn.loc.gov/2023044539
LC ebook record available at https://lccn.loc.gov/2023044540

For more information, write to Bearport Publishing, 5357 Penn Avenue South, Minneapolis, MN 55419.

CONTENTS

STRANGE TIME TO BE ALIVE

What was life like in ancient Rome? It was a peculiar past! At times, it could be brilliant, brutal, and truly **bizarre.**

Rome was founded in 753 BCE and became a powerful **empire** that stretched from Britain to Egypt. It lasted until the fifth century CE.

Today, ancient Rome is remembered for its impressive technology, rulers, and armies. But if you look closer, you'll find a much stranger story.

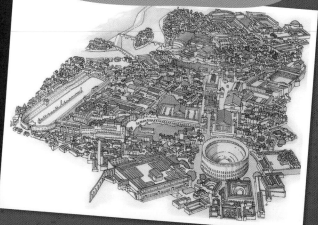

Even the **legend** of how Rome started is strange.

ROMULUS AND REMUS

This origin story tells of twin babies, Romulus and Remus, who were **abandoned** in the Tiber River. They were found by a mother wolf. She helped the boys, giving them food.

Remus

Romulus

Mars

When the twins grew up, they decided to start their own city. The brothers fought over what to call the new city. Romulus won and named it after himself. The city of Rome was born!

The story of the twins gets even weirder. They were said to be the children of Mars, the Roman god of war!

5

EMPERORS BEHAVING BADLY

For hundreds of years, powerful emperors ruled over Rome. A few of these leaders were truly odd.

Some of the strangest stories about Rome's emperors may be hard to believe. It is possible that certain stories were even made up to make some emperors look bad. True or not, these tales give us a pretty good idea of what ancient Romans really thought of their rulers.

Emperor Caligula

Emperor Nero

Emperor Elagabalus

EMPEROR CALIGULA

Emperor Caligula was very cruel to people. However, he treated his horse like royalty. The animal had his own **luxurious** stable, a fancy food **trough**, and a jeweled collar. The horse's oats may have even been mixed with flakes of gold.

Goats really get my goat!

Though he loved his horse, Caligula hated goats. Why? Caligula was a very hairy man, which made some people compare him to a goat. He made a law that no one was allowed to even mention the word *goat* around him. If they did, they would be killed!

Baah!

EMPEROR NERO

Emperor Nero didn't care about anyone but himself—not even his own mother. In fact, he tried to kill her . . . more than once! One time, Nero sent her out to sea in a leaky boat, but she managed to swim to safety.

Nero's mother, Agrippina

Nero liked to sing, and he loved to be praised for it. Nero even paid people to clap for his performances. He also made a rule that nobody in the audience was allowed to leave until he had finished.

One woman was forced to give birth to her baby during a Nero concert!

One story claims that Nero would not stop singing even as a terrible fire was burning Rome to the ground!

EMPEROR ELAGABALUS

Emperor Elagabalus came to power when he was only 14 years old. As emperor, Elagabalus got whatever he wanted. Some of his requests were rather odd.

According to the stories, Elagabalus had . . .

- A swimming pool filled with perfumed water
- Meals made up of food that was entirely one color, including a dish with a blue fish in an ocean-blue sauce
- A new pair of shoes to wear every time he left the house
- Golden pots for peeing and pooping in

JULIUS CAESAR

Rome's most famous ruler was Julius Caesar. He helped Rome take control of huge parts of Europe, Asia, and Africa.

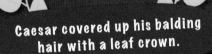

Caesar covered up his balding hair with a leaf crown.

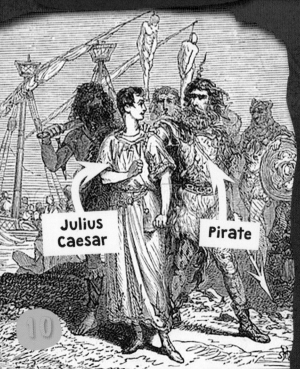

Julius Caesar

Pirate

During one of his journeys, Caesar was taken prisoner by pirates. They said they would free him if Rome paid a **ransom**. Caesar was **insulted** by how little money they demanded, so he made the pirates ask for more.

War wasn't the only thing Caesar was good at. He was also a gifted speaker. This helped him become a popular **politician**. At first, many liked Caesar, but then he got greedy. He wanted to stay in power for the rest of his life.

The other politicians were not happy with this power grab. They decided to kill Caesar. An angry group stabbed him to death!

Two of the people who killed Caesar were his friends, Brutus and Decimus. With friends like these, who needs enemies?!

CHICKENING OUT

What did the Roman army and chickens have in common? More than you might think!

Being a Roman soldier wasn't much fun. It involved lots of training, marching, and even the possibility of dying in battle. Some weren't up for the job.

I think I'd rather just join the army!

If soldiers chickened out during a battle, the punishment was harsh. Soldiers that ran from battle might be beaten to death.

One man tried to keep his sons out of the army by chopping off their thumbs so they couldn't hold swords!

A SIGN OF BAD CLUCK

The Romans had a strange way of guessing how they would do in battle. They believed chickens gave them clues about future success or failure. If the birds gobbled up food, it meant victory. If they ate nothing, bad luck was on the way.

When the chickens on one Roman warship refused to eat, an angry soldier tossed them into the sea. The Romans lost the battle soon after.

Let them drink, then!

The soldier really said this!

13

GUTS, GLORY, AND GLADIATORS

Fighting in Rome didn't stay on the battlefield. At the Colosseum, people fought for fame, freedom, and fun . . . well, the audience was having fun, at least!

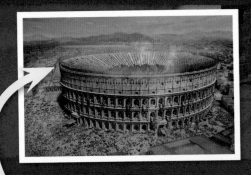

The Colosseum is a huge **amphitheater** where ancient Romans watched gladiators fight. Most gladiators were either **enslaved** or being held as prisoners. They were forced to entertain crowds by fighting one another and wild animals. Very successful gladiators could win their freedom. Those with less skill often died in front of the crowds.

Nearly half a million humans and over a million animals died at the Colosseum.

OUT OF YOUR HANDS

Even if you weren't the best fighter, there was still some hope for you. If you were defeated but still alive, the audience would vote on whether your opponent should kill you or let you live.

Audiences used their hands to signal their choice for life or death. A fighter didn't want to see a thumbs-down!

The final say on whether the gladiator would live or die was left to the emperor. Some emperors voted for life to show how **merciful** they were.

EMPERORS
IN THE ARENA

Gladiator fights were so popular that even emperors got involved.

EVEN EMPERORS CHEAT

Emperor Commodus liked to show off his fighting skills in the Colosseum. But his real skill was cheating. Commodus fought dangerous animals from the safety of a raised platform.

All kinds of animals were brought to the Colosseum.

Another time, Commodus killed what he said was a big, scary monster. But it was actually just a group of people tied together. They were armed with sponges painted like rocks!

Emperor Commodus

BOAT BATTLES

Sometimes, amphitheaters were filled with water so people could battle on boats. Emperor Domitian once organized a water battle that led to the deaths of every single fighter . . . as well as many members of the audience!

When a storm swept through the area, Domitian did not allow anyone to leave. People sat for hours in the cold rain. Later, many became sick and died.

SCARED TO DEATH

How else might you find entertainment in ancient Rome? By visiting the emperor!

EMPEROR DOMITIAN

Emperor Domitian once held a death-themed feast, complete with black decorations and black food. Each guest had to sit next to a gravestone with their own name on it. By the end of the feast, Domitian's guests were shaking in their sandals, convinced they would not leave alive.

Emperor Domitian

XII FLAVIUS DOMITIANUS.

GAIUS

Death-themed gifts were not unusual at feasts. Skeletons were often given to guests to remind them to enjoy life while it lasted!

Instead of killing his guests, Domitian sent them home with their gravestones. How thoughtful!

EMPEROR ELAGABALUS

Young Emperor Elagabalus loved to laugh . . . at other people. He sometimes pranked guests by locking them in rooms with his pet lions, leopards, and bears. Some guests dropped dead from fright.

One story tells of Elagabalus dumping tons of flowers on his guests, accidentally smothering some of them to death.

Some of Elagabalus's dinner guests weren't even given real food. They were served wood, stone, and wax instead. They had to pretend to eat while Elagabalus enjoyed a truly tasty meal.

DINNER AND A SHOW

Even feasts that didn't include pranks could still be pretty weird. The ancient Romans were all about making food fancy, even if that meant using odd ingredients.

Would you eat any of these Roman foods?

- Dormouse
- Jellyfish
- Sea urchin
- Giraffe
- Flamingo tongue
- Fish gut sauce
- Ostrich brains
- Camel heel

Can I interest you in an ice-cream sundae instead?

Want a snack? Try fruit, nuts, and . . . snails!

Leftovers from a feast

Ancient Romans ate while lying down on couches.

BORED AT THE BANQUET? NEVER!

A good Roman feast could last for hours. Luckily, there was often entertainment to go with the meal. Sometimes, you might even get to see trained lions and leopards.

Singers, dancers, jugglers, and fire-eaters also performed.

To really spice things up, you could have gladiators fight at your feast. Hopefully guests didn't mind a little blood spatter in their soup!

Marcus Gavius Apicius spent almost all of his savings on fancy things, such as throwing big dinner parties!

FOOD POISONING

Not everyone was a good dinner guest. Some would greedily gobble your food and down your drinks before trying to kill you! Poisoning enemies was popular in ancient Rome. To keep themselves safe, Roman emperors paid people to taste their food and drinks to make sure they weren't poisoned.

LOCUSTA, POISON PRO

A Roman woman named Locusta was an expert at making poison. She sold her deadly mixes to people looking to kill quickly and quietly. Even emperors hired her to poison their enemies!

Emperor Nero watched Locusta test her poisons on people.

YOU'D BETTER BEHAVE

Ancient Romans took crime and punishment very seriously, even if some of their laws were really wacky.

Here were some things that you were NOT allowed to do in ancient Rome.

- Wear purple (purple was for emperors only)
- Cry at a funeral
- Give someone who was killed by lightning a proper burial
- Write a mean or untrue song about someone

One emperor wanted to make a law that let people fart at the dinner table.

CREATIVE CRUELTY

Roman rules may have been strange, but the punishments were no laughing matter. If you broke the rules, you could be:

- Nailed to a wooden cross and left hanging until you died
- Tied into a leather sack with wild animals and chucked into a river
- Buried alive
- Thrown off a cliff
- Eaten by lions
- Stabbed with a large stick
- Sewn inside a dead donkey
- Stung to death by angry bees

To keep them from running away, prisoners were sometimes forced to wear uncomfortable wooden shoes.

CRAZY CLEAN

Romans kept themselves pretty neat and tidy. But the ways they cleaned themselves could be a little gross.

WHEN IN ROME, POO AS THE ROMANS POO

Public toilets were common in ancient Rome. People sat side by side on benches with holes cut out of the seat. They did their business with no dividers or stalls for privacy. Toilet paper didn't exist in ancient Rome. So, when you needed to wipe, you reached for a sponge on a stick.

All that waste piling up sometimes caught fire, sending flames through the holes in the benches!

BATHING WITH YOUR BUDDIES

Having a bath the Roman way meant taking a dip in a shared pool. Bath time was sort of a party. Baths were places where people met to chill and chat!

Ancient Romans sound pretty clean . . . right? Well, they also used pee to clean their clothes!

At the baths, you could ask to have the hair plucked from your armpits. This beauty practice caused people to scream so loudly from the pain that it bothered those living nearby.

RUDE ROMANS

Ancient Romans loved a good put-down.

For politicians, insulting one another was just part of the job. Being able to come up with the perfect dis showed that you were clever and good with words.

Your breath smells like my toilet sponge stick thingy!

Politicians were free to insult one another, but they were not allowed to make fun of ordinary people.

It wasn't just politicians who traded insults. Ancient **graffiti** from Rome shows that ordinary people insulted each other for all sorts of reasons.

Graffiti

Whoever wrote this insult on the wall of an ancient building in Pompeii must have been served a terrible meal there!

THE MONEY MANAGER OF EMPEROR NERO SAYS THIS FOOD IS POISON.

Even the walls themselves weren't safe from insults.

OH WALLS, YOU HAVE HELD UP SO MUCH BORING GRAFFITI THAT I AM AMAZED YOU HAVE NOT ALREADY FALLEN DOWN.

SERIOUSLY STRANGE

Ancient Rome was seriously interesting, even if it was part of a peculiar past. From brutal gladiator battles and ridiculous rulers to poison peddlers and bizarre banquets, ancient Rome sure had some terrible tales, surprising stories, and hard-to-believe history!